YOUR DESTINY:

Your Life and Your Work Become One

Robert Natiuk

YOUR DESTINY:
YOUR LIFE AND YOUR WORK BECOME ONE

First Printing: August, 1991.
Second Printing: October, 1993
Typesetting and Design by Image Factory, Santa Maria, California.
Printed by Publishers Press, Salt Lake City, Utah
Printed in the United States of America.

This book is lovingly dedicated to my wife, Martha, and my three children, Juli-Ann, David and Jonathan, who were my constant inspiration to work at home so I could be with them. They have made the effort very worthwhile and successful. Thanks, gang!

CONTENTS

Chapter

1

Do You Like Where You're Heading?

This is the story of three families.

Yet, it's also the story of millions of other families in our country.

Perhaps — you'll see yourself in this story.

LEO SMITH * . . . came from a small Texas farm. He was a hard-working, steady type of fellow who loved the outdoors and barbecues and country music. But as a boy, he saw how hard of a struggle it was on the farm. So, he decided to get a "secure job" instead.

In his mid-twenties, Leo went to work for a governmental agency. Then he married and soon was

*All stories are based on actual experiences but we've changed the names, or in some cases just used first names, to protect people's privacy. Also, we've avoided naming actual companies or products.

the father of two wonderful children. Even when the babies were still young, his wife had to get a job to "help make ends meet." That meant day-care for the kids and much less family time together.

Leo and his wife managed to get a few of those things that brought them pleasure — the camper and boat, a large color TV set, a compact second car. Life was good. At least — not bad.

Sure, at times Leo hated the regimentation of his job. At times his boss caught him daydreaming. Leo would have loved extra vacation time to go hunting and fishing more often, or take the kids somewhere special. But, there were the house and camper and boat and car and credit card payments!

"Boy, when I retire . . . !" Leo often consoled himself.

Because of cutbacks, at age 55 Leo was permanently laid off. For the next ten years he went from job to job. Then his social security checks started coming, and Leo tried retirement. But his income was too little. He found odd jobs. And, still dreaming of the hunting and fishing trips he'd take "someday," at age 67 Leo died.

Leo's story is not unusual. *At age 60, only five out of 100 people in the United States are financially secure.*

JOE NORTH . . . also was a hard-working, ambitious man who came from a poor family. So, in his thirties, Joe and his wife, Betty, saved up enough to buy a retail business in their home town. First — that meant tying up thousands of dollars in inventory. It also meant a couple thousand every month for overhead. That's why Joe and Betty worked six days a week, and sometimes seven, in order to make the business go.

Joe was a family man who dearly loved his children. "I'm doing all this for them!" he'd often assure himself. That meant missing many family times together — ball games and picnics and weekend outings. But Joe managed to put his children through a good college while wondering many times how they could grow up so fast!

Joe and Betty continued to work together and managed to build up some savings. After years of work, they were finally able to ease up a little. Until a discount chain store opened in their town.

Within a year Joe and Betty declared bankruptcy.

The hard years of work and the eventual insecurity made Joe morose and angry. He had no energy to begin again. In his early 60's, Joe died a disheartened man, leaving behind a grieving wife and children and grandchildren who never really had much

chance to know him and enjoy life with
him. **That's the saddest part of his story**.

**FORTUNATELY, THERE IS A HAPPIER STORY
I WANT TO TELL YOU ABOUT . . .**

DAVE SWENSON . . . had a lot of management
ability and was rising to the top in a department store.
But in his late 20's, Dave realized that his job was not as
challenging and secure as he would wish it to be. So,
he and his new bride, Linda, began a home-based
business in the health and nutrition field. They had
only *seven to ten hours per week* to devote to it. **But
Dave and Linda found that just seven solid hours
a week could accomplish a lot as they helped a few
other people achieve better health and a little extra
income**.

Within a few months, Dave and Linda were earning
an extra $200 to $300 each month, great for a second
car or saving up for an exotic vacation. *They also
gained important tax advantages*. And they loved
working closely with a few other couples like
themselves. *They found they were also developing
their personal talents — and that was their greatest
reward!*

Life to them became an exciting challenge. No
wonder they looked forward to each new day with
enthusiasm and expectancy!

When their part-time income surpassed their regular incomes, Dave and Linda quit their jobs and devoted "full-time" to their home business. *"Full-time" meant three or four days each week of high-quality time.* Often they could combine a vacation trip with their business and gain a tax deduction as well as relaxation!

WHAT DO DAVE AND LINDA LIKE BEST ABOUT THEIR HOME BUSINESS?

[ ] It costs very little to begin.

[ ] There is very little overhead.

[ ] Almost everyone can begin a similar business.

[ ] It doesn't require long hours — you can make your own schedule.

[ ] You don't have to leave your present job.

[ ] You get to know a lot of wonderful, exciting people with a purpose in life.

[ ] Achievement is based on talent and commitment — not race, sex, age or religion.

[ ] You have a lot of FREEDOM and UNLIMITED INCOME POTENTIAL.

[ ] You are truly in a people-helping-people business.

Now, check the benefits that appeal to you. And then ask yourself —

WOULD YOU LIKE THE KIND OF BUSINESS AND INCOME THAT DAVE AND LINDA DEVELOPED?

> **There's no reason why you can't have it!** Thousands of men and women from many different backgrounds have done it — doctors and truck drivers, nurses and waitresses, farmers, laborers, mechanics, lawyers, executives, artists, teachers and accountants . . . *and many others who've succeeded beyond their fondest dreams!*

I've seen people overcome shyness and personal handicaps. What you need is not necessarily a lot of talent, skills or time. *What you need is the DESIRE TO SUCCEED.*

You also need a network of capable leaders who are immensely interested in YOUR SUCCESS . . .

. . . AND THAT'S WHERE EXPERIENCE COMES IN!

In this type of home business, you will have a **guide or sponsor** who will work with you, provide you with training and direction and share success secrets with you. He or she will help you each step of the way.

YOU GET ALL OF THIS WITH VIRTUALLY NO COST TO YOU! Your sponsor or guide gets his commission from the company, not from you.

Do you want to be a part of this proven, exciting home business program? YOU CAN!

Already tens of thousands of people like you have said **YES!** Some are earning hundreds of dollars extra every month after just a few months. **Some are earning $1,000 to $10,000 per month. Some have surpassed that figure many times over. And they'll tell you they've just begun to achieve their potential.**

Just like them, you too might want financial independence . . . plus so many other worthwhile rewards: **personal growth — challenge — family togetherness — freedom to travel — exotic paid vacations and cruises — luxury cars — new friends — improved mental and physical well-being. And perhaps the greatest reward — THE KNOWLEDGE THAT YOU DID IT!** That you didn't have to wind up like Leo Smith, or like Joe and Betty North. That you will be among the five percent who achieve personal and financial independence.

What is your destiny? Where are you heading in life? Are you ready for **YOUR LIFE AND YOUR WORK TO BECOME ONE?** In your hands right now you have the key to your goals and dreams. Please read the rest of this book with an open mind. Perhaps what it offers is just right for you . . . perhaps it isn't. The decision is entirely yours. But you need the facts in order to make an intelligent decision. **That much you owe yourself.**

Now, the next chapter will highlight an attitude that allows you to be successful **immediately**, wherever you are. It is a principle of success that will empower you like nothing else can. If this attitude is an integral part of your life, you can't help but be successful.

**GET READY TO DISCOVER
"THE BIG STEP TO SUCCESS!"**

Chapter

2

Thankfulness: The Key To Natural Success

The title seems like such a simple idea, doesn't it? Can the **attitude of gratitude** really make all the difference in the world for your total success?

Cicero said: **"Gratitude is not only the greatest of virtues, but the parent of all the others."**

In order to own your own life, you must be thankful for who you are and what you have. The billionaire who isn't happy because he still wants more is not successful. Thankfulness can turn an ordinary meal into a banquet. *It's not what you possess that brings happiness — it's what you enjoy.*

It is this attitude which can help you become **FINANCIALLY FREE.**

Over the past ten years, I've interviewed and worked with many successful leaders in home-based businesses. Many of these people were earning over $100,000 per year. I asked, "What made these people so successful when others with equal or greater abilities didn't come close to such achievement? *What are the key principles in a successful home business*?"

The consistent thread through all these stories was thankfulness. That attitude carries us along the natural stream of success like a boat going along with the current. We don't have to fight to make headway. We go with the flow.

We naturally share with others what we're truly thankful for. We couldn't hold it back if we tried. It's an *overflow emotion*.

In any network marketing plan or home-business, the primary ingredient that leads to natural success is the product line or service. Not just "things" to buy and sell and use. But products or services with a **caring philosophy** behind them — ideas, products and services that **change people's lives for the better!**

We love working with people who feel this thankfulness happening within themselves. They energize us! We realize that they have a vision, a mission in life — they have an intense desire to create a better world, to share health-and-wealth truths with others, to contribute to the good of family, friends, country and Mother Earth.

> **People who are like this become OVER-FLOWINGLY THANKFUL. And like a waterfall, that has great power.**

It's this inner power that motivates so many leaders. First, the life-changing products or services they used for themselves brought many benefits. Then they couldn't help but share their experiences with others. They had to get the good news out to their family and friends.

PEOPLE WHO COULDN'T HELP IT!

Doug and Nancy Wilson were tired of trying to overcome their health problems through the standard medicines and drugs. They realized that they needed to take charge of their own health care. When someone introduced them to a health product line, they thought the concept made a lot of sense.

> But they made sure the distributor understood something clearly: "**We're only interested in the products. Don't bother telling us about the business!**"*

---

*All quotes are actual, with rare minor editing for clarity where necessary.

After all, Doug was earning a very good living as a hospital executive. And that took a lot of time.

The Wilsons found that the products helped them to overcome many of their health problems through better nutrition and lifestyle changes. When they talked to friends who also had health challenges, they naturally told them about their new program.

And that's the way they shared the idea — over and over again. It's called **word-of-mouth advertising**, very effective in "getting the message out."

That's how it worked with Doug and Nancy. They became distributors "just to get the products wholesale and share them with a few others." Those "few others" in turn shared the concept with others. Soon dozens, and then hundreds, of families were on that program. And many continued to purchase those products month after month because they found more energy and better health.

The first commission check Doug and Nancy received was for only a few dollars. The next one was several hundred dollars. By the sixth month, their check was over $1,000 — a nice second income. But because of the value of the products and the concept of rewarding those who do the promoting, the Wilsons' checks continued to grow for months to come.

Yes, there are many people who join a program because they want to tell others about the benefits; they have no other motive. When they start receiving checks for their person-to-person advertising, they're often surprised. That's what happened to Karen Peters. Vivacious and people-caring, she quickly became one of the top representatives in her company. Yet, financial rewards weren't in her mind when she first began. She said:

> "I didn't know I was starting a business.
> I was just sharing with friends!"

Wouldn't it be great to become **FINANCIALLY FREE** because you couldn't help it? *That's when your life and your work become one.*

FOR THE FUN OF IT!

> **Most people aren't looking for *more* work; but they'd definitely be very interested in MORE FUN!**

If your home-based business produces satisfaction and fun for yourself and others, you will attract many others to what you have.

Dr. Charles Millard, an emergency medicine physician, definitely didn't need more work. And he was earning enough money. But when he and his wife, Annette, looked at a home-business opportunity in the personal-care field, they saw a chance to work together and with other people. **"It looked like a lot of fun!" they said**.

They were right — it was fun! And the products proved to be valuable, helping people overcome skin, oral and home environmental problems very naturally. *Within 18 months, they were well on the way to earning an extra $10,000 per month.*

> Greater than the money, they admit,
> are the times they can spend together
> on achieving their goals, working
> with other couples and occasionally
> attending a company-sponsored
> leadership seminar.

In Colorado, Jo and Cal Simms are another couple who wanted more fun. Their tire store was profitable, but also "tiring"! One day a friend came by and gave them a few samples of some unusual personal-care products. The Simms loved those products, joined as distributors to get them wholesale and give a few samples to their customers and friends.

Now, after just a year of "part-timing" their distributorship, they plan to get out of the tire business entirely and enjoy their home-based business even more. Why? Because their part-time income now allows them to own their own life.

> Jo stated it this way: "**I love meeting people! It's a business that is a lot of fun. It also helps me to grow personally. And we help others like us to find a better lifestyle**."

FOR THE JOY OF IT!

Of course there will be challenges to meet, discouragements to face in your home business, like in any other worthy endeavor. What will keep you going? It's the joy you experience from helping others and from developing your abilities.

A couple from Michigan said it well: "There are so many people in this country who need help physically and financially! All we need to do is turn around and we will find someone who needs our help."

> "**The KEY is to find these people and let them enjoy the health-and-wealth opportunity we have found. The results they receive will get them excited and this enthusiasm will naturally excite others. If you excite others, you can't help but be a success**."

Another couple experiencing that same kind of excitement are Marvin and Geneva. He's a former college sports coach and knows well the value of motivating people.

> "We share with people an understanding
> of health, nutrition, and financial
> stability. Not a day goes by without us
> talking to at least one person about
> our health program. Most people are
> sincerely interested in better health,
> making our job very enjoyable."

The simple truth: The more people you help achieve their worthy goals, the closer you'll come to achieving your worthy goals. And you naturally share with others what you're truly thankful for. Your story flows from within — you couldn't hold it back even if you tried. Thus, it's true: **WE DON'T SELL — WE SHARE!**

Too simple? Too idealistic? Doesn't work in the real world? I believe the next chapter will set the record straight as you discover how these principles have brought great success to others.

Chapter 3

Success Through
The Power of
Inner Marketing

Sometime ago, I packed away most of my books on salesmanship. I wanted to write a book showing people how to succeed at marketing without having to become sales people. What I discovered is something much more powerful than salesmanship.

THIS IS THE PRINCIPLE OF ATTRACTION.

Become the kind of person you want to attract. Become healthier. Become more vibrant and energetic. This does not come by pretending to be enthusiastic or by trying to follow some rules of positive thinking. Rather, it comes through a caring attitude for yourself, your family and others.

Michael and Adina Rudin have that kind of transforming attitude. Michael was a medical doctor in eastern Europe before coming to the United States in 1980. But he couldn't practice in this country.

"When we came here, we didn't even have enough money to buy proper winter clothing," he related. "And in New York City the winters can be cold! Now we own four condominiums worth half a million dollars."

How did they do it? By developing a home-based business in the health field. "We started our business with $24 and lots of enthusiasm. The products we used for ourselves made us look good, and that made us feel good! People wanted to know what we were doing. Many people love to come to our seminars simply for good company. And we care about them, their dreams, their goals. We know it's possible for each one, no matter how poor, to achieve what we have achieved. We want to help them do that."

> **The Rudins didn't sell a thing; they**
> **followed a lifestyle that made**
> **them healthier and better looking!**
> **They attracted others who saw**
> **and wanted the same thing.**

THAT'S INNER MARKETING! You're simply being yourself, **but *your self*** is alive with **hope, health,** and

joy. And hundreds of people you meet will want that
same kind of self.

People will see that *your life and your work are becoming one*. You're not dependent on medical professionals, bosses, or the government to direct and improve your life. *You are in charge of your life.* This doesn't mean you are an island, sufficient by yourself. Rather, you might recognize that your strength and guidance depend on a Spiritual Power. You realize that other people are very important to you and in your personal growth. You have an *attitude of humility*, *of gratefulness*, rather than of haughtiness. **This is a teachable spirit.**

> You want to learn from others so you
> will have more to teach others.

> You want to share with others because
> you're thankful that others have shared
> with you.

> You have a GOOD CAUSE to live for.

These principles bring about INNER MARKETING. And inner marketing is a natural force that is much more effective than sales techniques. That kind of inner power comes from being involved in a great cause.

WHAT IS A GREAT CAUSE?
You are!

That's right — in the best sense of a home-based business, you are ultimately building yourself. Your family, loved ones and friends are an extension of yourself.

> **This attitude — that YOU ARE YOUR
> BUSINESS — is really one of the greatest
> steps to personal growth and success
> you can ever realize.**

This attitude says that you are successful because you are following the way of thankfulness and right principles, working from a center of integrity. You are growing into being the best you can be; you care for other people more than you care about achieving the trappings of what the world considers success to be.

I can best illustrate this through the story of two of my close friends and associates, John and Sharon. I've known them and worked with them for seven years. What they say comes from the heart.

For many years, John and Sharon struggled to make their apple orchard profitable. That took many years of hard work and many hardships.

Early in their marriage, Sharon faced some serious health challenges. She started on a long road to learn for herself which natural healing methods could help solve those health problems. This gradually led her to sharing her knowledge with others. Eventually, she found a company that fit in very closely with what she was doing. She used that company and its products as the basis for her home-based business.

It took only a few months before John and Sharon's business was profitable. Now, seven years later, their earnings surpass **$50,000 per month.** Not only that, they've helped hundreds of others build businesses of their own.

This is what Sharon says: "**Service first, then prosperity. The money will come through the back door. Money is nothing more than a measuring rod of service.**"

This couple's business philosophy is really a philosophy of life: "**Honesty, integrity and learning are the keys to success. Misrepresentation must be avoided. Building people is vital.**"

And here's their key to success — *it is the power of inner marketing:* "**You cannot sell anything effectively unless you are sold on it yourself. Success comes through a true desire to help others. This is a commitment to a worthwhile cause.**"

Some marketers call this "being a product of your product." But that is just a part of the truth.

Inner marketing comes from being a product of a lifestyle, which may include certain health and personal development products.

Several years ago I interviewed two young women who were partners in a home business in the health field. When I talked with them, I could sense the power of the emotional commitment they had made to a high-quality lifestyle. Their faces lighted up with confidence that was almost irresistible.

> Nancy summed it up thus: "You've got to believe in what you're doing. We always felt we were doing much more than building a business for ourselves. We felt we were also contributing to a bigger objective, that of helping people to ease some of the hurt of the world."

> Her partner, Sibyl, said: "It's impossible to be happy while being selfish. If you live your life for others, and if you think of others, happiness will come to you."

Too idealistic and impractical for the real business world of today? Not when your business is yourself. Over and over again, people like Nancy and Sibyl and John and Sharon and the Rudins have proven — *you can be idealistic, love the work you do, and make a very good living.*

PEOPLE POWERED FROM WITHIN

Here are some quotes from people who have built home-based businesses netting them over $100,000 per year.

Don and Jan: "You must be emotionally and intellectually honest with people. You can't present something as being good when it isn't. Our company and product line have that kind of integrity; therefore we love to share it with others."

Don and Jan became millionaires within a few years through that kind of home business.

Barbara: "If you're sold on the products, believe me, you will never have to sell anyone."

Barbara is one of the top achievers in an internationally known health and personal-care company.

Robert and Carol: "Our central goal was to have a lifestyle that would allow us freedom to be successful as parents, to spend extra time with our children. Freedom to us means helping others gain financial independence. We ask ourselves — Are we really living up to our talents? Are we helping people change their lives for the better? Do we truly have the love in our hearts that we need?."

Robert and Carol have developed a million-dollar-a-year income by helping others to achieve their personal and health goals.

David and Ann: "There is great satisfaction and joy in helping others to achieve a happier, healthier and more rewarding lifestyle. We're still amazed when we think that we started this business for less than $100, and yet we've been able to build a business by sharing these concepts and teaching others."

In just a matter of a few years, David and Ann have found greatly improved health and wealth through their own home-based health/personal-development business.

WHAT IS THE POWER BEHIND
THESE PEOPLE'S SUCCESS?

INNER MARKETING. When you feel that power taking form within you, you'll *naturally* start doing the right things to share your business. You'll just be yourself — but it will be a self that wants to share the best with everyone!

Chapter

4

The Best Reasons
In the World

What are some main reasons why motivated people like you join a home-based network?

Let's consider just a few of them. As you consider these, you might want to jot down what would be important to you.

INCOME

This concept gives you an opportunity to earn that **second income** at your own pace, during hours you can most easily invest. A business like this can also provide you with a **primary income** that has no limits. You can also save money by being able to purchase life-enhancing and highly effective products and services at wholesale. Plus, you could easily earn additional rebates.

YOUR OWN BUSINESS

You have the security and satisfaction of building your own business with a very small investment. You can grow at your own pace, and no one can fire or hassle you. **You are truly your own boss.** That means — **YOUR LIFE AND YOUR WORK BECOME ONE.**

LOVE OF PEOPLE

To be successful in this business, you have to love people. You will deal with a variety of people as you build your income. You will learn to better understand all kinds of people and grow to love them more. Yet, you can also **CHOOSE** the people you want to work with. **You *choose* your associates.** That is both a challenge and a reward.

Remember that you are not in the direct-selling business. *You are in the people-building business.* That means you find out what people's needs are and, wherever you can, you help them find a way to fulfill those needs.

WORK WITH FAMILY

Our home-based business concept can bring a family together in a mutual project that benefits everyone. Husband and wife often form a close-knit team. Children find ways to help too. Everyone in the family can participate in goal-setting and working to achieve those goals.

EXPAND YOUR CIRCLE OF FRIENDS

Many of your associates will become close friends. You will find your **circle of influence** widening. You will constantly come across new opportunities to meet interesting people.

EQUAL OPPORTUNITY

Your education, religion, sex, race or background will not hinder your progress as a home-business builder. Basically, everyone has the same opportunity. **You will be rewarded solely on your performance**.

BEST OF BOTH WORLDS

You can stay at your present job, business or profession as long as you wish. You need risk nothing when you become part of a home-business network. You likely will miss an occasional TV program **because you'll find challenges that are much more interesting and rewarding!**

You can build a bright future for yourself and others with an investment of just seven to ten hours per week. Some have done it with less. You are not rewarded for HOW MUCH TIME you put in but on **HOW WELL YOU USE YOUR TIME.** That skill will also spill over into other areas of your life, enabling you to be generally more efficient and productive. **In short, what we offer you is an environment where you "learn on the job," but that job can lead to life's richest rewards, including career security and financial independence.**

JUST LIKE THE PARABLE OF TALENTS

Some people use their abilities and reap a profit. Others bury their abilities and lose what they have. The first group finds life to be fulfilling and exciting. The second group often finds life boring and a drudgery.

"IF IT IS TO BE, IT IS UP TO ME!"

That's the motto of the talent-developer! You are reading this book **because you know it's up to you to**

become what you want to be. If you decide to be part of a vital home-business network, you'll be associating with others with that same attitude.

You belong in a life-enhancing network **IF** — you want to achieve a powerful but balanced life . . . you want freedom of your time . . . you want to strive for the highest life has to offer . . . **YOU WANT A CREATIVE BALANCE OF WORK AND LIFE. That is your destiny.**

YOU WANT INCREASED TAX ADVANTAGES!

Your own business can provide you with some of the best tax advantages available to the average family.

One word of warning — keep good records and consult with your tax counselor or accountant. There are important guidelines set by the Internal Revenue Service (U.S.A.) or Revenue Canada which you must be aware of in order to qualify for rightful deductions.

WHAT YOU CAN DEDUCT

Automobile expenses — for all business-related travel. You can deduct either the costs of depreciation, upkeep and fuel, *or* you can deduct a certain amount per mile traveled.

Office in your home — With certain stipulations, you can deduct a portion of your mortgage interest, property tax, utilities, maintenance, improvements, depreciation, and other expenses. Ask your Internal Revenue Service for the publication, "Business Use of Your Home."

Business travel — air fares, portion of meals, taxi, lodging, etc., connected with your business trips.

Telephone bills — All your long-distance calls connected with your business are deductible.

Family partnerships — can lead to significant tax savings through income disbursements, retirement plans, etc. You might check into incorporating your business for additional savings.

Seminars, conventions and training programs — You can pursue self-development programs in relation to your business and deduct most costs.

Miscellaneous — samples, postage, bad debts, depreciation of office and business equipment, advertising, promotional costs, interest on business indebtedness, insurance, legal and professional services, office supplies and repairs, rent, when connected with your business can be tax deductible.

The IRS and Revenue Canada have dozens of publications that can guide you in record-keeping for your business and tax purposes. Or, you might want to work with an accountant who is experienced in this field.

MORE THAN TAX SAVINGS

Some companies and home-business promoters stress the tax-savings angle when promoting their company, showing how a person can increase his spendable income by one or two thousand dollars through their part-time venture. Although in some instances this may be true, **we recommend that you become involved in a home business for more important and substantial reasons** — added income and self-development.

The tax savings are there, but they are meant for the business person who is seriously interested in developing a *profitable* business. They are not meant to be a tax shelter. They are connected with legitimate expenses and deductions in connection with your business.

THERE IS ONLY ONE WAY —

To succeed in your home-based business — you must choose a company or concept that is a winner!

You could do all the right things — spend plenty of time working and learning — and yet fail *IF* your business is based on false principles or a weak idea.

In the next chapter, we're going to cover **the principles of successful home-based businesses**. These principles when applied to your choice will greatly increase your chance of success.

You want a fair chance to succeed because you deserve that chance.

GET READY TO CHOOSE A WINNER!

Chapter

5

Choosing
A Winner

"The world makes way for the man
who knows where he is going."

Ralph Waldo Emerson

When you've decided to develop your own home business, what do you look for? What are the guidelines to guarantee success as much as possible? **How do you choose a winner so that YOUR LIFE AND YOUR WORK BECOME ONE?**

We'll provide answers to these important questions. These answers come from experts in the field of business. They're time-tested and will help you better define what you should look for.

I suggest that you carefully consider what you read in this chapter as it applies to your options. Your intelligent decision can make all the difference in your life whether you become financially independent or continue to be dependent on a boss, a company or others who make the decisions as to how much you'll get paid for what kind of work and for how long.

MORE THAN A LIVING

"Making a living" is a common phrase to describe one's work.

But most people forget what is vastly more important.

"**Making a life!**" Most people want something more than just a good income. People who are "making a life" want to enjoy what they're doing with such a great part of their time.

Many people think that the way to a happy life is to make a lot of money. But they spend so much of their time making enough money that they don't have any time left to enjoy it.

Is having a business of your own the way to have plenty of **time and money**?

TIME FREEDOM

People who begin businesses on their own usually "want to make a lot of money." But for most, there is more to that explanation. *They want to earn enough income so they can have more time to enjoy life*.

What happens? Most owners put in 60, 70, even 80 hours per week to make their businesses work. So, they don't get what they really want — **TIME FREEDOM**.

When the average business owner figures out his investment, time and energy, the dollar-per-hour income is very small.

This raises the question: What is the difference between **financial independence** and **financial freedom**?

FINANCIAL INDEPENDENCE — means you are producing your own source of income. You are *independent* for your finances. But in order to do that, you might be locked into a 60-hour week, have all the headaches of employees, inventory, overhead, regulatory paperwork, and more.

FINANCIAL FREEDOM — means you have **TIME FREEDOM**. You can spend your days the way you wish, and still have enough money to pay the bills.

The mountain hermit who needs $100 per month to get along and has an income of $150 per month is financially free. The business owner who needs $12,000 per month and earns $11,999 per month is not free. The person who earns $250,000 per year and can't "afford the time" to take a vacation with his family is not free. The person who is trading his health, family and social life for financial security is not free.

You want to discover how you can be both FINANCIALLY INDEPENDENT AND FINANCIALLY FREE.

But first, you must ask yourself the right questions and get the right answers.

ASKING THE RIGHT QUESTIONS

I've spoken with hundreds of people who got into a business of their own without asking enough questions and getting solid answers. Often, they've been moved by emotion, by a few facts, by the promise of a large income in a short time. Sometimes, they've been influenced by family, friends and business associates.

To make a wise choice, however, you need more. You need to ask the right questions. Marketing consultant Richard D. Smith has spent many years researching home-based businesses and asking questions. He's also gotten hands-on experience by developing several businesses for himself.

Richard also brings to his questions many years of sales leadership in one of America's largest pharmaceutical companies. He's a respected and much-in-demand teacher of salespeople, network marketers, multi-level marketers and home-based business developers.

Now, here are Richard's criteria with which you can measure a good home-based business opportunity.

1. **QUALITY. Are the company's products and/or services of highest quality?** You want to be proud to be a representative.

2. **VALUE. Are these products or services *priced right*?** Can they stand up against the competition? Will people feel they are getting their money's worth?

3. **NEED. Is there a *natural demand* for these products and services?** Will users *want* to tell others about these products and services? Do the benefits far outweigh the cost? Will most users "fall in love" with the products? Will there be repeat purchases?

4. **PROFIT. Does the company reasonably reward their representatives?** Does the marketing plan

generate a long-term and increasing income? Can most adults *actually* do it? Are people actually earning significant money after six to 12 months? Can you achieve substantial income levels by working with just five or six people? Can people build it who are not retailers or professional salespeople, who don't like selling?

5. **INVESTMENT. What are the risks involved?** Will you need a large inventory? Does the company allow reasonable time for someone to back out and get his money back? How much money could someone lose if the program didn't work for him? Would you be placing others at financial risk?

6. **LEADERSHIP. Does top management have the necessary experience and skills?** Do the leaders have a sense of mission, purpose, commitment? Are they people-centered? How much debt are they carrying and what is their line of credit? (If the company is debt-free, so much the better.)

    How complete is their data processing service for controlling internal procedures? What ongoing information will you be getting to help you plan your business?

    Does the leadership have impeccable standards of integrity? Have they proven themselves in the marketplace?

7. **SELF-DEVELOPMENT. What kind of training and educational tools do they offer?** What is the cost? Are they constantly developing improved material, and is it reasonably priced?

Do they offer ego-satisfying and motivating incentives? Are a large number of representatives finding satisfaction in being trained and do they feel they're growing into becoming more and more capable?

8. **TIMING. How long has the company been in business?** Has it not only survived but become stronger during those first few crucial years? Has it experienced steady growth? Has it shown flexibility in making necessary changes and improving what may not be perfect?

Is the company about to enter the rapid-growth phase? Or, is that explosive stage passed or too far in the future? Some companies have already peaked and some new ones are too weak to experience rapid and solid growth.

Does the company and its philosophy, product line, leadership, etc., generate within you goals, dreams, emotions, desires to achieve and succeed? If so, likely the timing and the company are right for you.

THE ONLY GUARANTEE

There are years of wisdom and thought in the above checklist. I recommend you use it as you explore any business opportunity, including what friends and relatives might offer you.

If a company meets the above criteria well, can you be guaranteed financial success? No — for there are no such guarantees in life. There are other variables.

If you decide to develop a home business, you'll want to focus on time-tested and people-centered concepts. Don't be persuaded by promises of easy and quick riches. No one can guarantee that you will be financially free in six months, or even six years. But by following the right principles, you can at least have the guarantee of increasing your abilities, knowledge, clarity of thinking and circles of influence.

The home business that's right for you should help you develop in your social, communication, time management, and other personal skills. *You will be able to take what you learn and be more successful in many other fields.* And that means that you will have a much better opportunity to secure **FINANCIAL INDEPENDENCE AND TIME FREEDOM.**

How do you begin? By thoughtfully considering the next very important section of this book. This is the time to consider *YOUR DESTINY:* **HOW TO HAVE A CAREER YOU LOVE.**

Chapter

6

Choosing
A Winning Team

Destiny is not a matter
   of chance,
it is a matter of choice;
it is not a thing to be
   waited for;
it is a thing to be achieved.

William Jennings Bryan

Too many people shy away from a home-based
business of their own because they fear they'll have to

do it by themselves. A lonely struggle. Great odds. Long hours. Years of learning and re-learning.

After all, who is going to help you succeed anyway?

YOUR TEAM.

That's right — in a people-centered program you have a team that wants to see you succeed, reach your goals, realize your dreams.

On your side, you could have the dedication and experience of dozens of others. First, there is your sponsor.

TEAM MEMBER #1 — YOUR SPONSOR

This concept goes back a long way. **Webster's Dictionary** defines it thus:

> "**Sponsor** — one who presents a candidate
> for baptism or confirmation and undertakes
> responsibility for his religious education
> or spiritual welfare . . . one who assumes
> responsibility for some other person."

This intriguing concept reminds us of the craftsman-apprentice relationship. The professional would take a young person into his place of business and, over a period of several years, teach that youth everything he knew about the craft.

It is an awesome responsibility to be a sponsor! You take upon yourself the welfare of another person, at least in some area of life. You become their "**surety**" or "**guarantor**," synonyms for "**sponsor**."

In a networking type of home-based business, you should get a sponsor who will be your "surety of success." That sponsor will commit himself to helping you succeed, matching your commitment. Simply put, this means there are at least TWO PEOPLE devoted to your business success — you and your sponsor.

BUT WHY WOULD A PERSON BE *YOUR SPONSOR*? Because there are still some people who truly want to help others. There are also personal rewards — a sense of achievement, leadership development . . . **and FINANCIAL REWARDS.**

This, in turn, encourages you to sponsor others like you have been sponsored. You do this quite naturally because you have something good to share.

> **When you represent a company that markets its products or services through the network system, then you will earn *an override commission on that person's production*.**

I think of my sponsor in the health/personal development program which my wife and I have worked for eight years. Yes, we've earned tens of thousands of dollars in override commissions for him. But he in turn has traveled across North America, holding training meetings for the people we've sponsored. He's been on the phone countless hours and sent out many letters. He is a good sponsor.

But he's not the only one on our team!

TEAM MEMBER #2 — YOUR SPONSOR'S SPONSOR

Sharon sponsored the man who in turn sponsored us. She has been an exceptional help in our nationwide network. She travels a lot, holds terrific seminars, sends out a very helpful monthly newsletter, and talks a lot on the phone! Without her help, our job would've been much harder. She in turn is being paid by the company for her efforts in helping build up people. And her income has grown to tens of thousands of dollars every month. Her motto:

> "The more people you help achieve
> their goals, the closer you'll come to
> achieving your goals." That's a net-
> work home-based business at its best.

So, too, Steve and Penny illustrate this concept very well. They enjoy helping people become healthy through their products. "It's hard work to educate people, start them on a road to natural healing and then encourage them through their ups and downs," they explain. "But when someone achieves success, the job is well worth it and we feel satisfied that we've helped as much as we can."

A POWERFUL PRINCIPLE
OF SUCCESS IS YOURS!

J. Paul Getty, one of the world's richest men, once said:

> "There are three things necessary to achieve financial wealth:
>
> 1. Own your own business.
>
> 2. Have a product or service that people want or need.
>
> 3. And, have a system that allows you to duplicate yourself through others."

Those are exactly the principles we follow in building a home-based business in the health/personal development field!

Helping you build that business could be your sponsor's sponsor's sponsor . . . and so forth. But there are even more people on your team.

TEAM MEMBER #3 — YOUR ASSOCIATES

If you're with an exciting company that is helping to change people's lives for the better, you'll find a camaraderie with many others in that company. People who may never financially benefit from your efforts will often go out of their way to help you. People you sponsor will feel at home in seminars and networking groups anywhere in the nation. And you in turn will feel it a privilege to invite others into your networking activities. **Everybody wins as everybody shares their knowledge and experience.**

TEAM MEMBER #4 — THE COMPANY

The leaders of the company you represent know that their success depends on the success of people like you. Therefore, a good networking company will have ongoing training seminars, sales aids, marketing and personal-growth tools.

But above all, their products or services must change people's lives at a fundamental level!

Several years ago I sponsored James in Pennsylvania who in turn sponsored John in Massachusetts. Both of these young men first got excited because of the products.

> **"The products are so good I got in-
> volved," John related. "It takes an
> incredible product to create the
> right opportunity."**

Now, John's nationwide network is incredible — over 20,000 people! His income is exciting. And instead of driving the beat-up car he used to have, he now owns two Mercedes-Benzes, both awards from the company.

**YOU NOW HAVE ENOUGH FACTS . . .
MAKE THE RIGHT DECISION FOR YOURSELF.**

A network-type of home-based business may not be for you. But right now over 5,000,000 people have discovered it. And that number grows by thousands every day. Over $10,000,000,000 worth of products and services are marketed by these people every year. Those who've joined a solid company and became leaders earn thousands of dollars every year. Some earn hundreds of thousands of dollars.

Was it easy for these leaders to achieve those rewards? Of course not! But it was worth it. These people found — **BETTER HEALTH OF BODY AND MIND . . . TIME AND FINANCIAL FREEDOM . . . JOY IN THE PRESENT AND HOPE FOR THE FUTURE.**

Follow the right principles — choose a company that meets your high standards — become part of a dedicated team and work together. My friends, John and Marilee, said it well: "One of the biggest rules of making money is to understand that those who are financially independent are OWNERS, not LOANERS. Find a networking company that gives you the opportunity to be an owner at very little or no risk."

AND YOU'LL FIND YOUR DESTINY:
YOUR LIFE AND YOUR WORK BECOME ONE!

Chapter 7

Choosing
Winning Trends
For Success

**If you continue to think
like you always thought
you'll continue to get
what you always got!**

Anonymous

Perhaps you're saying, "Sure, this home-based business is all right for some people. But not for me. I'll wait for something else to come along."

What else?

A winning lottery ticket? A rich relative who leaves you his million-dollar estate? A job promotion that lifts you to financial security?

Sure — those kinds of lucky breaks happen . . . rarely. But 99% of us will have to create our own fortune. *And the best way you can do that is to flow with the trends.*

For instance, some people made fortunes in real estate in the 1970's and 1980's. The trend was toward rapidly increasing prices. But in the 1990's that trend reversed itself and prices started dropping. To buck this trend and try to make your fortune in a market where the demand is weakening would be very risky.

Why not discover the major trends for the 1990's and go with those? GO WITH THE TYPES OF BUSINESSES THAT TAKE UTMOST ADVANTAGE OF THIS DECADE'S MAJOR TRENDS. If you use those trends to your advantage, you'll develop your business and income much faster and much more easily.

Let me assure you — in the very near future — just a matter of six months to two years — *you can have the kind of financial security and time freedom that you've dreamed about and wished for.* A home-based business that goes with the major trends can give you that.

YOU'LL HAVE A BUSINESS THAT —

- requires no office or storefront, *very little overhead!*

- you can easily build with only 7 to 10 quality hours per week

- brings you important tax benefits generally available only to business owners

- rewards you with better health, more vitality, improved abilities, and much, much more!

IS IT WORTH YOUR EFFORT?

Christine, with a B.S. degree, had been a full-time dental hygienist for over 20 years. As a single parent of two children, she didn't have much time for a second business. But when she learned about a network marketing company in her field, she became very interested, joined and found rewards beyond her initial expectations.

> "My primary focus was on my personal development. This philosophy has given me the freedom and security I've always strived for but really never experienced before. After just two-and-a-half years of part-time effort, my monthly commission checks *exceed my full-time income!*"

JUST THINK —

- no more daily commutes — painfully early mornings to get to work in some busy office or depressing work place

- no more 49 to 50 weeks of hustle and hassle for a few weeks' vacation

- no more unrewarding monotonous tasks day after day

- and if you're in a regular "storefront" type of business, you can get rid of the mounds of paperwork and profit-draining overhead!

Sounds too much like a fantasy, an unrealistic dream? Let me tell you about Dennis.

In his twenties, Dennis was severely injured in a car accident. The doctors told him, "You'll never be able to work again. You might as well resign yourself to welfare."

But Dennis and his wife, Jenny, did not accept that verdict. Instead, they started looking for what they could do from their home. They began by investing their entire bank account — $16.00 — in a home-based business in the health field.

> Within a year, their net income was over
> $4,000 per month — and growing!

I know of dozens of other inspiring stories like that. There's the story of Marilyn, a widow in her late fifties. Soon after her husband died, she exhausted the little bit of life insurance and savings she had. She desperately hunted for some kind of job to make ends meet. But at her age she couldn't find anything.

Marilyn started a home-based business in the health and personal-growth field. **And within only five months' time, she was earning over $3,000 per month!** The really neat thing was that she did it by helping a lot of other people toward better health of body and mind.

I've interviewed other families who've developed even higher incomes. **In fact, some are earning $10,000 to $50,000 per month. Many accomplished this part time. Some have retired and their income keeps coming in!**

WHAT IS THE SECRET?

> You want a business where you have a
> large number of people helping you —
> WITHOUT having them on your payroll!

Of course, these people get paid for their efforts also. *But the same company that pays you pays them!* You have very little paperwork, no worries about workman's compensation, employee benefits, disability insurance and all the other hassles of the business world.

Yet, your income can grow to equal that of the top business leaders in today's corporations!

Robert, in his early forties, lost everything he owned in the construction business — his home, his equipment, his savings. But he never lost his faith in himself and the love and support of his family. Eight years ago he began building a home business in the health and personal-growth field. Today, his income is close to a million dollars per year . . . and growing!

> *Robert's Rule-of-Life:* "When you really think about it, you're investing in yourself. Your greatest asset is yourself. You are building up your home business, which is really an investment in your life. Most people spend more time planning their vacation trips than they spend planning their goals in life."

Ah ha! A get-rich-quick scheme! Not at all. **What I'm talking about is proven 100% by thousands of people like you.** Yes, a few of these business-builders started earning thousands of dollars per month within a few months. But most of them developed their income week by week, month by month, growing at 5 to 10 per cent per month.

My wife, Martha, and I began a home business eight years ago. Since we both were involved full time in our professions — I as a writer and Martha as a musician — we only had a few hours here and there for our new business. Our third month's income was $200. Nothing to brag about but all right for our time investment. By the end of the second year that part-time income was over $2,000 per month. In the third year we were earning over $5,000 per month, still part time, and we had earned a bonus car, a new Volvo 760.

Our income has continued to grow steadily until today we earn more per month than most families earn in a year. We can retire if we choose to. We can travel and meet the many friends we've made in almost every state and throughout Canada. We often take our children with us on exotic vacations. We find joy in being able to contribute to child-care organizations and other worthy causes.

We didn't develop such a rewarding income just because of our time or talents. We found a program that, like a pendulum, swung with today's major trends. That gave extra impetus to our efforts and helped our business grow rapidly.

When you follow our recommendations, you'll swing with at least three of the major pendulums of the 1990's . . . and even into the 21st century. **YOU'LL HAVE TRIPLE MOMENTUM FOR YEARS TO COME THAT'LL HELP TO PROPEL YOU TO FINANCIAL FREEDOM!**

TREND #1

Millions of people recognize that *they need to do something to take control of the source of their income.* That's their only real security. They also recognize the need for more opportunities to take advantage of legitimate tax deductions.

Therefore, they need a business of their own. **In fact, one out of three families *wants* to start their own business.** All they need is a proven business program that is very simple and inexpensive to begin.

Every week, thousands of people like you start on the road to developing their own home-based business. **THIS IS A MAJOR TREND IN TODAY'S WORLD. GO WITH IT!**

TREND #2

Another really major pendulum swinging in your favor is *the trend toward taking control of one's own health care.* You see this in the rapid growth of health spas, exercise programs, books and articles on nutrition and health improvement. TV and radio programs have greatly increased their time for talk shows on health. Along with health, more and more people desire to improve in mind and spirit.

A large percentage of today's people have recognized that their health and well-being is in their own hands. And they're ready to do something about it.

> Health, nutrition and personal development make up a BIG PENDULUM that swings in favor of your financial freedom. Why not take advantage of this major trend?

TREND #3

It's called **NETWORKING**. This is the sharing of our abilities and knowledge with others for everyone's benefit. It's working together through a spirit of co-operation, not competition.

Health, nutrition and personal development have always worked well through small groups "networking" their knowledge, skills and products. These groups are sources for shared wisdom, for encouragement, for helpful personal experience.

NETWORKING is a "MEGATREND" that can help you become financially free through your home-based business. And you can feel good about this achievement because along the way you'll help hundreds, perhaps thousands, of people find a better way of life.

HOW ABOUT PUTTING TRENDS #1 . . . #2 . . . AND #3 TOGETHER?

Exciting? You bet! Profitable? Thousands of people like you have proven it over and over again.

Here's what Susan, an actress and homemaker, says about building a business that helps others:

> "The personal growth and training I have received in my network marketing program has helped me to redesign my entire future. I'm already ahead of schedule for financial freedom. I'll have a million-dollar business in two more years!"

Perhaps Nancy Anderson, a career consultant, writer and editor, sums it up the best:

> "When your life 'works,' your life comes together, with a harmonious balance among all its facets: your work, your family, your loves, your finances, and your mental and spiritual growth."

WORK WITH PASSION, p. 1

The Vision and Power Are Yours

"The best idea in the world is valueless until you take action on it — today, not tomorrow."

Napoleon Hill

Now — for the steps you need to take to achieve your dreams!

It's not my purpose in this book to cover every step in a successful program, or acquaint you with all the tools, seminars, audio and video tapes, reports, associations, and much more information that is available to help you **"grow a home business of your own."** You'll learn about these success tools soon after you've teamed up with a good sponsor.

RIGHT NOW — THE BIG QUESTION IS —

Do you really want what hundreds of
others have experienced? A solid plan
for financial freedom. Better health.
A livelier mental attitude. Room for
personal growth. An opportunity to
challenge your abilities.

DO YOU REALLY WANT YOUR LIFE AND YOUR WORK TO BECOME ONE?

In her excellent book, **WORK WITH PASSION**, Nancy
Anderson writes:

"When you are doing the work you love,
all else in life seems to fall into place. When
you do well in your life's work — whatever
that is — you feel well. Your sense of
personal worth is keen, and you then see
the personal worth of others. **It is through
the dignity of the work we do that we
achieve self-esteem in life**" (page 9).

Marsha Sinetar in her book, **DO WHAT YOU LOVE,
THE MONEY WILL FOLLOW**, speaks about the unify-
ing power you will feel when your work, love and play
become a cohesive activity. She calls this "the right
livelihood." And that comes about when you are in a
type of work that develops your total being.

"If people cultivate self-respect and inner security and develop a commitment to their own talent, they can earn as much money as they need, or want. This is true success . . . it means to go beyond the goal of money to the goal of authentic self-expression, self-trust and actualization" (page 6).

Why aren't more people happy in their work? Because, according to a recent national poll, 95 percent of America's working population do not enjoy the work they do!

The famous novelist, John Gardner, wrote: "The best-kept secret is that people want to work hard on behalf of something they feel is meaningful, something they believe in."

You can find a home-based business into which you can throw your heart, mind and body without reservation. Perhaps, at first, you can do this for ony five hours a week. But you'll have that activity to look forward to. It'll be your special incentive for the whole week, something that livens up your dreams, keeps you going through any tough week. You will have hope for the future as, step by step, you build your own business.

DO YOU REALLY WANT YOUR LIFE AND YOUR WORK TO BECOME ONE?

For most people, there's no better way to do that than to develop a home-based business in the health and personal-growth field. Whether your main concern is better health, or meeting pressing financial challenges, or finding freedom to be your own boss, or expanding your involvement with people — you can find the answer in a proven lifestyle business.

YOU SAY — SELLING IS NOT FOR YOU

"But I could never sell anything!"

Often I've heard that reason given by someone who is learning about a home-based marketing business.

My answer: "That's the greatest advantage you can have!" It's a startling answer that comes from my own experience.

Working my way through college, I spent a few summers trying to sell children's books door to door. That is — when I got to the door! Many mornings I would circle the blocks . . . or the farms . . . trying to find courage to knock on that first door. And when I finally did — sometimes after several hours of just traveling — I prayed that no one would be at home.

Sometimes, though, someone was at home. And sometimes I got in and made a presentation. Sometimes I sold some books. But when I didn't, it was back to wandering the streets and roads, trying to find courage for the next rejection.

I didn't join a health-oriented company because I loved to sell! I joined to get the products wholesale. And when those products began to change my life for the better, and the lives of others, I found that my fear of selling started to disappear. I found myself wanting to tell others what I had found!

Building a successful home business doesn't mean selling day after day to a lot of people. It means —

1. Use the products for yourself. Become a product of the product.

2. Share the benefits with others without even trying to persuade them to buy. If they feel a need for results similar to yours, they'll ask questions.

3. They might do more than buy the products. They might join your company and start sharing with others. And you'll receive ongoing commissions.

If you knew about products that could help your friends or family get better health, more energy, clearer thinking, would you naturally tell them about those products?

Were you selling something the last time you told your friends about a great movie you saw, or a wonderful restaurant you ate at? The majority of people go to new movies and restaurants, not because of advertising, but because friends told them how good these were.

This is called "word-of-mouth" advertising. But you usually don't get paid for it.

However, in your home-based business you can build a very profitable income from sharing something good with a small number of people.

Some people call this type of business a "multi-level marketing program." That means you tell someone who tells someone else who tells still others. You might tell five of your friends how good the movie was, and they see it for themselves. They like it and they in turn tell five or so friends. That means you've directly and indirectly influenced 30 people to see that movie. If the theater had paid you $1.00 for each person, you would've earned an advertising commission of $30.00, which would have more than paid for your ticket.

I call this type of business *personal network marketing.* Often it is chosen, in one form or another, by caring people who deeply believe that they can contribute something good to the lives of others. In actuality, they are **people-builders** rather than **sales persons.** They have a mutual goal with their prospects: to encourage the development of potentials and a better lifestyle.

Today, there are an increasing number of major companies who have seen the power of word-of-mouth advertising and are paying commissions to their "advertisers," or distributors.

Another modern term for this type of distribution system is called **NETWORK MARKETING.** In many of these systems, you can build a strong network starting with *just four or five people* you sponsor as distributors or members. You then help these four or five people sponsor others.

How do you find those five people? Some might already be in your network of friends, business associates or acquaintances. You'll find others by doing what you like to do — going to social functions, attending health and personal-development seminars, spending time with friends, and generally becoming more interested in life and others.

YOUR POWER TO MULTIPLY YOURSELF

In a network or multi-level program, you build your business through the process of multiplication, not addition.

In addition, you add people one at a time. For instance, if you had a successful storefront business and wanted to expand, you'd add more staff or a branch store — one at a time. That costs money and consumes much effort.

But in network marketing, you *sponsor* your associates, who in turn can sponsor others, and so forth.

If you sponsored five who in turn sponsored five each, you'd have —

$$
\begin{array}{rl}
5 & \text{sponsored by you} \\
\times\, 5 & \text{sponsored by each of your five (average)} \\
\hline
= 25 & \text{on your second level}
\end{array}
$$

You'd have a total of 30 associates in your business — five on your first level and 25 on your second. As these people buy products from the company, you'd likely be earning commissions or overrides.

Let's take this further, as many of today's companies do.

25	on your second level
× 5	sponsored by each of above (average)
= 125	on your third level
+ 30	on your first and second level
= 155	associates in your business.

Let's say that each one of these associates ordered $100 worth of products every month.

$100 × 155 = $15,500.

And you averaged 5% commission override on those purchases. **$15,500 × .05 = $755 commission each month**. Not bad for a part-time effort with just five associates you sponsored. Let's say that you continue to add qualified associates on your first level until you have a team of ten.

10	on your first level
× 10	sponsored by each of above (average)
= 100	on your second level
× 10	sponsored by each of above (average)
= 1000	on your third level.

Now, in your network you have 10 + 100 + 1,000 for a total of 1,110 associates. Each averages $100 product purchases for a total of $110,000 product sales in your organization, on which you average 5%.

That would be a monthly commission of $5,550. Even though you've only doubled the number of people you've personally sponsored, your eventual commissions could multiply many times. In this illustration, five associates multiplied on three levels produced $755 commissions. But ten multiplied on three levels produced **$5,550 commissions.** That's the power of multiplication in network marketing!

Many companies pay more than 5%. And some pay to the fifth level or more.

Notice that you didn't concentrate on selling products, but rather on showing a handful of people a process of doing business — ordering for themselves and sharing that opportunity with others. You don't have to be a salesperson but rather an encourager — someone who likes to share good things with others.

This type of marketing, or sharing, comes from a spirit of love rather than gain. You love what you're doing and want others to join you.

> **"First law of money: Do what you love; the money will come if you follow your heart. I'll add that you must do it *long enough*."**
>
> **WORK WITH PASSION, p. 87**

Move On and Up
To Success

Debbie A. Ballard, president of an international consulting company in network marketing, defines success this way:

> "Personally, I look at success as feeling good about how I'm progressing towards my own goals, while maintaining a happy, balanced life.

> "It's a course I set for myself, a way of life filled with both achievements and the inevitable, momentary setbacks I view as opportunities to learn, develop and grow.

"When you cultivate an attitude for
success that's realistic, that's all yours
and isn't based on anyone else's
definition, that attitude itself will help
keep you on a success track."

> MLM SUCCESS
> October 1990, p. 21

All well and good so far. But perhaps in your mind
there's one big problem —

YOU DON'T AGREE WITH NETWORK
OR MULTI-LEVEL MARKETING!

Very understandable. There have been many
programs which called themselves "multi-level
marketing" and weren't. They were pyramid schemes
or direct sales. And there are some programs which are
multi-level marketing but are not people-centered.

Because network/multi-level marketing has
changed so much during the last five years, it's important for you to take a fresh look at it.

But it's even more important to carefully check out
the particular program presented to you. There are
worlds of differences among the successful network
marketing programs today. Likely, there are a few

that will suit you much better than others. Some are still in the horse-and-buggy days as far as their distribution system is concerned. Others are highly sophisticated, very solid, financially among the top 500 companies in North America.

The good company has a long-term business plan, not a "get-rich-quick" scheme. Distrust any plan that tries to manipulate you into fast action with hyped-up deadlines. If someone tells you, "You must get in now to make the money," don't get in. A good program will be just as good, perhaps better, several months or years from now.

Look at a company without prejudice, judging it on its own merits.

First . . . are the products valuable to you and others?

Second . . . is their marketing program fair and proven?

Third . . . does it have high-caliber leadership?

It wouldn't be fair to you to judge all network companies by that one or two you investigated some years ago. Nor would it be fair to judge some of today's high-integrity companies by some of the flaky fly-by-night operations disguised as multi-level marketing companies.

You might also know of some people who tried this home-based business idea and worked hard and didn't get anywhere. Of course, I know of cases like that too. And in most of them, the problem can be pinpointed to one simple fact —

THEY CHOSE BUSINESSES THAT DIDN'T FLOW WITH TODAY'S TRENDS

- unexciting, non-progressive product lines that didn't change people's lives dramatically

- marketing structures that forced them to re-distribute goods and pay commissions out of their checks

- leadership that wasn't centered on training their business builders to grow and share with others

- a high-pressure, unrewarding marketing plan

That's why sound recommendations for your own business are based solidly on programs that have proven themselves and that are growing fast because they fit this decade's strongest trends.

When you swing with the pendulum of a strong trend, you have momentum in your favor. If you try to buck that pendulum, you are bound to lose. It's as simple as that.

I believe you'll become very excited when you investigate some of today's proven companies. After doing so, you might think: "This is so much different than I pictured! I'd have no problem building a business with this company!"

Simply put —

> **CHOOSE A COMPANY YOU'D BE PROUD TO TELL YOUR FRIENDS ABOUT** . . . **even if you didn't make any money by doing so! Why? Because you want to see others receive the benefits this company offers, whether from the products or the marketing plan or both.**

CHOOSE A COMPANY THAT MATCHES YOUR VISION

Bob Henrie, an international marketing consultant, lists four qualities for a business to be outstanding in today's world.

1. **It must be a company that is in tune with today's trends.** Today's people want a better lifestyle, better health, longer-lasting youth, control of their income.

2. **It must be a company that is unique**. It sets itself apart from all others. You cannot get excited about a "me-too" type of company. But you can get enthusiastic about a company that has a unique place in the world.

3. **It must be a company with a vision**. It should have the guts to step into the world with progressive ideas, with principles that will change lives for the better for years to come, with a desire to change the world for good.

4. **It must be a company that encourages personal growth**. You do not pursue wealth; you grow into wealth. When you share good, you get good back. The more people you're able to help, the more you get in return. This type of wealth includes more than money; it includes friends, development of talents and skills, family togetherness, spiritual qualities, and more.

John Naisbitt said it well in his remarkable book, MEGATRENDS: "In the network environment, **rewards come by empowering others, not by climbing over them**."

When you attend a convention of network marketers in a good company, it's really thrilling to see people helping each other and sharing their "secrets of success." Most times, you'll find a spirit of humility, even among the top achievers, for the best of net-workers recognize that they owe their growth to many others. This depth of mutuality overrides hyped-up competitiveness.

> "You'll know your flower patch is right
> when you sense the pleasant growth
> of yourself; you are glad to be learning
> what you are learning and you like the
> other flowers around you."
>
> WORK WITH PASSION, p. 8

In this type of atmosphere, you are bound to discover and clarify your values, your life's purpose and mission. And that in turn gives you a sense of in-vigorating wholeness.

> "When you are doing the work you love,
> all else in life seems to fall into place. When
> you do well in your life's work — whatever
> that is — you feel well. Your sense of
> personal worth is keen, and you then see
> the personal worth of others. *It is through
> the dignity of the work we do that we achieve
> self-esteem in life.*"
>
> WORK WITH PASSION, p. 9

"You will be satisfied." Do you sincerely want your life and your work to become one? What you do for a living is helping you to live your life to the fullest. And then you share that fullness of joy and satisfaction with others.

You can very likely discover this satisfaction through your own home-based business. Others have. Why not you?

Randell Anderson is a very successful network marketer with over 20 years' experience in that field. His motivation is his love of people, wanting to see the best for them.

> **"People are emotionally and financially starving out there, partly because we've gone into such an automated, computerized, automatic teller-and-pay-your-bills-by-phone type of society. Network marketing is so attractive because we're going back to the feelings of family. We care — for ourselves and for our people — and we get paid for doing it. We get in tune with ourselves. Then we find that's intensified by sharing ourselves with others."**
>
> **MLM SUCCESS**
> **January 1991, p. 6**

"Thinkers" and "Clunkers"

Simply put, "thinkers" are statements, facts or events that make you think about something very important to your life. Here are some "thinkers" for you to wrap your brain around for a while!

REASONS TO CONSIDER NETWORK MARKETING FOR YOUR HOME-BASED BUSINESS

1. **You don't need to invest your savings or borrow large sums of capital to get started.** The upfront cost to start a franchise can be considerably over $100,000. And even for franchises, the failure rate in the first five years is over 80%. But with a sound network company, you can start for less than $200.

Nor do you need to quit your job or undermine your security in any way. You can start part time and work your way into a full-time business. Or, you might continue with your present work or profession or business and just develop your network business for a residual or second income. It is up to you entirely.

2. **You can work out of your home**. You need no expensive overhead, which is a killer in new storefront businesses. Your family can also be involved.

3. **You can own your own life in terms of being your own boss**. You schedule your time and resources as you wish. This allows you to dream your big dreams and create your future by directing your abilities according to your time schedule.

4. **You reap what you sow**. You prepare the soil, plant, water and tend and harvest. Your earning potential is virtually unlimited. Your income for the first few months might be only a few hundred dollars. But then you could see it grow to a thousand, then several thousand. After a year or two, your income could be ten thousand per month or more.

5. **Your business can keep on growing *even if* you take it easy in a particular month.** You could take a long vacation, come back and discover that your check has increased. Why? Because you'll have others building the business even in your absence. This is not a one-time commission arrangement. You'll have a monthly repeat business with a residual income.

6. You'll discover many other rewards besides financial — personal growth, opportunities to serve others, etc.

7. You can earn extra money to supplement your current income, or you can replace your current income.

8. You can affect the lives of many others with improved financial and personal health.

9. **You'll have freedom to enjoy your lifestyle.** You'll have control of your business rather than your business having control of you.

10. You don't need a large inventory since your associates can order direct from the company.

11. Your life and work will be toward solutions, not problems. Network marketing is more than a business; it is also a family.

12. You'll be learning principles of a regenerative life. You'll learn not only the **how's** but also the **why's**.

13. You'll be in business for yourself **but not by yourself**. Company leaders and trainers as well as people in your network will contribute to your success.

14. Your opportunities for travel will increase, both for business and for pleasure. Or, if you choose, you can build your business locally and avoid travelling great distances.

15. At least 20 percent of North America's work force operate part- or full-time out of their home. By the year 2000, that is expected to increase to over 30 percent. Home-based businesses are increasing at 7.5% per year — or over 1,000,000 new ones each year.

●   ●   ●   ●   ●

CLUNKERS — deal with the way things are but most people avoid thinking about them because the truth hurts.

"CLUNKERS" ON THE ROAD TO FINANCIAL SECURITY OR RETIREMENT

1. In the 1980's, 87% of Americans 65 years of age or older lived on less than $10,000 per year! Yet,

most of these families had earned more than $1,000,000 in their working lifetime! The trend of the buying power of the average wage-earner's income in 1990 and 1991 has been downward.

2. At their present income level, only 5% of Americans will be able to attain financial security — if they budget and invest their earnings wisely for 30 to 40 years and don't face any extreme hardships and reverses.

3. Fewer than 1% of Americans ever achieve their dream of financial freedom.

4. A Gallup poll revealed that —

   • only 41% hold jobs they had planned

   • one-third of the work force expects to change jobs within the next three years

   • one-half of Americans say job stress affects their health, personal relationships and their ability to do their job

   • 65% would start all over if given the chance

5. "We choose . . . or others choose for us."

6. To depend on your investments for a comfortable retirement, you'd need to have $500,000 to $1,000,000 saved. That's in today's economy. Ten years from now, with inflation and increasing taxes, you'd need at least twice as much.

7. Over **90% of new businesses are out of business within 5 years**. In network marketing, you are developing yourself as your business. As long as you're improving your resources — your abilities, skills, knowledge, communications, relationships — you're adding value to your business. **You never fail as long as you are improving your business (yourself) and never give up!**

8. Most people who are dissatisfied with their work have a **JOB** — which stands for **Just Over Broke!**

9. Really think about this one:

   When you get to where you're going, will you be where you want to be?

   - Take charge

   - Take control

   - Take a chance

It is wonderful to discover who you are; it is more wonderful to decide who you will be.

"He put his hand upon my shoulder
and told me that in the world were
two kinds of people, those who wish
and those who will, and the world
and its goods will always belong to
those who will."

Louis L'Amour in The Warrior's Path

Will you?

_____

SELECTED RESOURCES

BOOKS

Anderson, Nancy. WORK WITH PASSION. New York: Carroll & Graf
Publishers, 1984.

Babener, Jeffrey and Stewart, David. THE NETWORK MARKETER'S GUIDE
TO SUCCESS. Scottsdale, Arizona: The Forum for Network Marketing,
1990.

Covey, Stephen R. THE 7 HABITS OF HIGHLY EFFECTIVE PEOPLE.
New York: Simon and Schuster, 1989.

Davidson, Jeffrey P. AVOIDING THE PITFALLS OF STARTING YOUR OWN
BUSINESS. New York: Walker and Co., 1988.

Edwards, Paul and Sarah. WORKING FROM HOME, revised ed.
Los Angeles: J. P. Tarcher, Inc., 1987.

Failla, Don. HOW TO BUILD A LARGE SUCCESSFUL MULTI-LEVEL
MARKETING ORGANIZATION. Gig Harbor, Wash., 1984.

Kalench, John. BEING THE BEST YOU CAN BE IN MLM. Encinitas, Calif.:
MIM Publications, 1990.

Naisbitt, John and Aburdene, Patricia. MEGATRENDS 2000. New York:
William Morrow and Company, 1990.

O'Connor, Lindsey. WORKING AT HOME: The Dream That's Becoming
a Reality. Eugene, Oregon: Harvest House Publishers, 1990.

Peale, Norman Vincent. POWER OF THE PLUS FACTOR: The Little Extra
That Makes You a Winner! Carmel: New York: Guideposts, 1988.

Pike, Thomas and Proctor, William. IS IT SUCCESS? OR IS IT ADDICTION?
Nashville, Tenn.: Thomas Nelson Publishers, 1988.

Pride, Mary. ALL THE WAY HOME. Westchester, Ill.: Crossway Books,
1989.

Sinetar, Marsha. DO WHAT YOU LOVE, THE MONEY WILL FOLLOW:
Discovering Your Right Livelihood. New York: Dell Publishing, 1987.

Williams, Art. PUSHING UP PEOPLE. Doraville, Georgia: Parklake
Publishers, 1985.

MAGAZINES AND NEWSLETTERS

Entrepreneur, 2311 Pontious Ave., Los Angeles, CA 90064.
(213) 478-0437.

MLM Success, 310 East Main St., Suite 310, Charlottesville, VA 22901.
(800) 927-2527, Ext. 656.

Opportunity Connection, P. O. Box 57723, Webster, TX 77598.

Money Maker's Monthly, P. O. Box 7116, Villa Park, IL 60181.
(708) 920-1118; FAX (708) 920-8377.

ORGANIZATIONS

BioResearch Foundation/Tapestry Press, P.O. Box 658, Springville. UT
84663. Phone: (800) 333-4290. Offers books, booklets, tapes, videos
and seminars in achieving top-level health, personal development and
financial freedom.

GAGE RESEARCH, 7501 E. Treasure Dr., Lobby Floor, North Bay
Village, FL 33141. Phone: (305) 864-6658; (800) 432-GAGE. Recruiting
tape **"Escape The Rat Race"**; network development tapes and live
seminars.

Home business Resource Center, P.O. Box 115023-233, Carrollton, Tx
75011. Publisher of a newsletter called **Home Work**. Provides
resource information and books written from a Christian worldview.

MLM International, Inc., P.O. Box 889, Gig Harbor, WA 98335.
(800) 458-0888; FAX (206) 851-3069. Variety of books, cassettes and
videos to help you build your home-based networking business.

National Association for Home-Based Businesses, P.O. Box 30220,
Baltimore, MD 21270. Phone: (310) 363-3698. Resources for creating
home businesses in many fields; also offers seminars on starting and
developing your business.

Success-Line International, P.O. Box 31995, Seattle, WA 98103.
(206) 284-1730; (800) 735-1035; FAX (206) 286-0495. Markets business
stationery, seminars, books and other material for home-based
businesses.

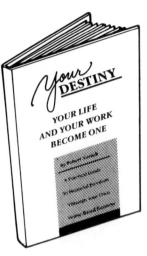

SIMPLIFY YOUR BUSINESS.

SPEED UP YOUR RESULTS.

SHARE **YOUR DESTINY** WITH YOUR FRIENDS AND PROSPECTS!

You can easily help others catch the vision of financial freedom and personal growth. Just share copies of **YOUR DESTINY**. This book can help inspire and instruct others as it has inspired you.

Now, you can order extra books at wholesale prices. If you wish, resell these books at a profit . . . or just lend or give copies to those favorite people in your life and to other key prospects. Either way, you'll be doing them a favor.

You can order extra copies at the following discount prices:

NUMBER OF BOOKS	PRICE PER BOOK (U.S.A. Funds)
1	$7.00
2-5	$6.00
6-11	$5.50
12-20	$5.00
21-50	$4.50
51-119	$4.00
120-239	$3.50
240 +	Please call for quote

SHIPPING AND HANDLING

Inside U.S.A.: Add 7%.
Minimum: $5.00 per order.

Canada: Add 10%.
Minimum: $7.00 per order.

Overseas and special orders:
Actual shipping charges.
Washington state addresses:
Please add applicable sales tax.

CREDIT CARDS: MasterCard and Visa Accepted

MAIL ORDERS: Harmony Media
17714 - NE 110 Ave.
Battle Ground, WA 98604-6119

PHONE ORDERS: (206)687-3435; (800)488-7343

TO LEARN MORE

It is not the purpose of this book to recommend any particular network marketing program but only to direct you to the best principles in choosing one that fits your needs. **You must accept the responsibility to find the right home-based business for yourself — that way your life and your work can become very much your own.**

If someone gave you this book, your first step would be to get in touch with that person and find out more.

Thank you for seriously considering how you can improve your life and that of others.

For further information, please contact: